OVER 100 *CLEAN & ORIGINAL* JOKES...A TENTH ROUND

Copyrighted

Over 100 *Clean & Original* Jokes...A Tenth Round
Text copyrighted by Jake Duzan
Cover illustration copyrighted by Jake Duzan

I hereby that the following jokes are original and they were written by yours truly, Jake Duzan. Any similarities to names, places, or events is purely coincidental.

JOKES

Why did the doctor hesitate before giving the patient medication for his itchy skin?

Why did the doughnut crème filler quit after his tube ran out of icing?

What did one knuckle say to the other after it was popped?

Why did the snowball travel alone on its way to the ground?

Why was the customer hesitant to buy the pillow

case at half price?

What do you call Tapioka on crackers?

Knock! Knock!
Who's there?
It's Summer
It's Summer who?

Knock! Knock!
Who's there?
10-4
10-4 who?

Knock!   Knock!
Who's there?
Woody
Woody who

Where do swine keep their money?

Knock! Knock!
Who's there?
Bean
Bean who?

Why did the out-of-towner take directions from the
hand puppet?

Why didn't the city dwellers think the big hand on
the town clock was accurate?

Knock! Knock!
Who's there?
Roger
Roger who?

How long have the eskimos been cold?

Why didn't the old man at the retirement home
bring his walking stick to the going away party?

What did they say about the karate student who kicked the window and shattered it?

Why did the TV show about a broom do so well?

Knock! Knock!
Who's there?
Wes
Wes who?

Knock! Knock!
Who's there?
Sal
Sal who?

Knock! Knock!
Who's there?
Tim
Tim who?

Knock! Knock!
Who's there?

Adam
Adam who?

Knock! Knock!
Who's there?
It's Autumn
It's Autumn who?

Knock! Knock!
Who's there?
I'm Gary
I'm Gary who?

Knock! Knock!
Who's there?
I'm a lion.
I'm a lion who?

What did you call a roll on a moving coaster?

What is yellow, has three eyes, and eats yellow corn?

What kind of records do they listen to in Heaven?

Knock! Knock!
Who's there?
Theodore
Theodore who?

Knock! Knock!
Who's there?
I'm Max
I'm Max who?

Knock! Knock!
Who's there?
I'm Cindy
I'm Cindy who?

Knock! Knock!
Who's there?

I, Doug
I, Doug who

What is the possum's motto?

Knock! Knock!
Who's there?
Wayan
Wayan who?

Why wasn't the kitten allowed in the stockroom?

Knock! Knock!
Who's there?
Greg
Greg who?

Why were the two socks inseparable?

What did the cooks call the egg whose shell allowed them to see the yoke?

Why did the man give up on trying to lose his belly fat?

What did the cooks say the egg was doing when it fell out of the fridge and roamed all over the floor?

How did the female puppy react when it got a bad manicure?

Why did the man cry when he cut the onion?

Why didn't the bird want to fly with the other bird?

Knock! Knock!
Who's there?
R.U. Stali
R.U. Stali who?

Knock! Knock!
Who's there?
Just us
Just us who?

Knock! Knock!
Who's there?
Lynn
Lynn who?

Knock! Knock!
Who's there?
Atlas
Atlas who?

What did they call the man whose jacket fell into
the sugar bin?

How do you celebrate hamburger beef that passes inspection?

Knock! Knock!
Who's there?
Eve
Eve who?

Knock! Knock!
Who's there?
Stu
Stu who?

What is the philosophy of the bee?

What do you call a dog that can tell time?

Knock! Knock!
Who's there?
Indy

Indy who?

Knock! Knock!
Who's there?
It's just Don
It's just don who?

Knock! Knock!
Who's there?
Mel
Mel who?

Knock! Knock!
Who's there?
Less
Less who?

Knock! Knock!
Who's there?
Marv
Marv who?

Why didn't the chef want to use the weird-shaped egg?

Knock! Knock!
Who's there?
Walker
Walker who?

Knock! Knock!
Who's there?
Hank
Hank who?

Knock! Knock!
Who's there?
A. B.
A. B. who?

Knock! Knock!
Who's there?
Plum
Plum who?

Knock! Knock!

Who's there?
Vulcan
Vulcan who?

What do you call a bunch of bees following behind
a leader?

Knock! Knock!
Who's there?
Brock
Brock who?

Knock! Knock!
Who's there?
Cain
Cain who?

Why didn't the film noir do so well in the movie
theaters?

What kind of tropical fish never goes to the "ocean
bank"?

Why couldn't the queen bee find the worker bee?

What did all the people say about the huge dust storm?

Knock! Knock!
Who's there?
Soda
Soda who?

What was the excuse the surgeon gave for not wanting to do a surgery after driving through four towns using only back roads to get to the hospital?

Knock! Knock!
Who's there?
I'm Darrin
I'm Darrin who?

What did the powers that be on Mars put into place

to keep their inhabitants in line?

Why did the comedian "branch out" in his comedy
routine?

Knock! Knock!
Who's there?
I'm Mona
I'm Mona who?

Knock! Knock!
Who's there?
14 Karat
14 Karat who?

Why was the mollusk so heavy?

Why did the servant give the king a bowl of peas
for dinner?

Knock! Knock!
Who's there?
It's a critter
It's a critter who?

What did the head master at the boarding school say to the nun when he thought she was lying to him?

Knock! Knock!
Who's there?
I'm Ann
I'm Ann who?

Why was the clothing designer so confident that his line of dresses would do so well?

What did the witness say about a group of vigilantes that were forced by the mafia to go around spray painting all of the mail boxes in the neighborhood?

Knock! Knock!
Who's there?
Cory
Cory who?

Knock! Knock!
Who's there?
Y.O.Y.
Y.O.Y. Who?

What did the wooden puppet say when its master
said it would never talk by itself?

Knock! Knock!
Who's there?
N. Case
N. Case who?

Knock! Knock!
Who's there?
I'm Mo
I'm Mo who?

Knock! Knock!
Who's there?
Person at door shows sign through window that reads, "Larry".
"Larry who?"

What did they say about the egg that "came out of its shell"?

Knock! Knock!
Who's there?
A hun
A hun who

Knock! Knock!
Who's there?
High five
High five who?

Knock! Knock!
Who's there?
Hoss

Hoss who?

Why was the sea otter surrounded by so many people?

Knock! Knock!
Who's there?
Eel
Eel who?

Knock! Knock!
Who's there?
Wayne
Wayne who?

Knock! Knock!
Who's there?
It's Di
It's Di who?

What do you call a puppy that can't speak?

Knock! Knock!
Who's there?
Bye
Bye who?

PUNCHLINES

Because he didn't want to make a *rash* decision.

It just wasn't fulfilling anymore.

I'm getting out of this joint.

Because it was such a flake.

Because something told him that it was a sham.

Puddin' on the ritz.

It's summer now.   I've been standing out here since Spring. Can you let me in?

Ten for you, a ten dollar bill, if you let me in!

Wood (would) he or you let me in!

In a piggy bank.

Bean (been) out here for a while. Could you let me in?

Because it had *first hand* knowledge.

Because it was *second hand* information.

Roger that.   We need confirmation that we can

come inside.

Since brrrrrrrrrrrrrrrrrrrrrrrrrrrrrrth (birth).

Because there was no *staff* allowed!

"He really kicked gl-ass."

Because it was sweeps week.

Wes-tern cowboy here. Could I come in for a spell?

Sal-ivating, I'm salivating out here. Could you let me in so I could get a drink of water?

Tim-pting (tempting), isn't it? I know you wanna let me in!

Adam-ic (atomic) radiation is everywhere outside.
Can I come in?

It's Autumn now. I've been standing out here since
Summer, now let me in!

I'm Gary-nteeing (guaranteeing) you that you
won't regret it if you let me in!

I'm a lyin' (lion) out here, waiting for you to open
the door!

A roll-er coaster.

A yellow three eyed yellow corn eater!

Di-vinyl records!

The-odore-able (The adorable) decorations out here are nice, but I'd appreciate it if I could come in!

I'm max-in' and relaxin' out here, just waiting for you to let me in!

I'm Cindy-ng (sending) flowers to you...from a friend. Could you open the door so I can give them to you?

I Doug (dug) a hole into your basement because you wouldn't let me in!

"Anything's possum-able!"

Wayan (why in) the world haven't you let me in already?

It didn't have enough *e-kitty* (equity).

Greg-arious person on your doorstep. Can we chit chat for a while?

Because they were *soul mates.*

EGGS-posed (exposed).

Because it was such a big waste (waist).

It was EGGS-ploring.

She was *apawed* (apalled).

Because it had a bad op-onion (opinion) of him.

Because the bird *tweeted* the other bird badly.

R (Are) U (you) stali-ng (stalling) or something? Could you let me in?

Just-ice (just us) of the Peace here. Did somebody here want to get married?

Lynn-d (lend) me your time and your ears! I want to come inside!

At-last! I'm here. Can you let me in?

Sugar coated.

You give it a *com-mince-meat* (commencement) ceremony!

Eve-ning, sir. Aren't you going to invite me in?

Stu-pendous house you have here. Can I come in?

"To bee or not to bee, that is the question."

A watch dog.

Indy-pedent thinker from Indiana. Could I come in and discuss the state of the world today?

It's just Don-ning on me...that I've been talking to you for a minute and you haven't invited me in.

Mel-low out, dude, and let me in!

Less-see (Let's see) if you'll let us in!

Marv-elous to see you! Could you let me in?

Because he didn't EGGS-cept it.

Walker on over to the door and let me in!

Hankerchief (handkerchief)...I have a handkerchief handy...do you need one? Sounds like you might have sneezed!

A B C...now that I know my A B C's, won't you open the door for me?

Plum-ber here. Havin' some trouble with your toilet? I'm gonna have to come inside and take a look.

Vulcun-o (volcano) just erupted behind me! Help! Lava everywhere! Can I come inside?

Its BEE-sciples (disciples).

Brock-oli (broccoli) for you if you let me in!

Cain (can) I come in?

Because it was ig-NOIR-ed by all the critics.

The cheap skate (skate is a tropical fish that looks like a sting ray).

Because she couldn't locate what BEE-partment he belonged to.

"It was the darn *dust* thing."

So, duh, are you gonna let me in?

"I just completed four bypasses!"

I'm Darrin' you to let me in!

Martian law.

Because he was tired of the same old *schtick* (stick).

I'm mona'n (moan-in') and groanin' because you won't let me in!

14 karat-e students on your doorstep and we're gonna karate chop you if you don't let us in!

Because it had so much *mussel*.

He wanted to ap-PEASe him.

It's, uh, critter-cal (critical) that you let me in!

"That's NUN-sense!"

I'm Ann-ouncing right now that I think you should let me in!

Because he sWORE by it!

"It was black mail."

Cory-ographer (choreographer) here and I would like to put you in my next rock video. Could I come inside and discuss it with you?

Y (Why) O (oh) Y (why) haven't you let me in already?

"Knock on wood."

N (In) case you didn't know, I would like it very much if you would let me in!

I'm Mo-wing everybody's lawn in the neighborhood for a small price...maybe I can come in so we can discuss the details?

Person at door shows another sign that reads, "Larry-ngitis, terrible case of Laryngitis. Can't talk. Could I come in?"

Very EGGS-istential.

A hun-dred dollar bill for you if you let me in!

Hi! Five dollars for you if you let me in!

Hoss-pital (hospital) ambulance outside.   We'll
need to come inside!

They wanted its OTTER-graph.

Eel-even (eleven) dollars for you if you let me in?

Wayne (when) you gonna let me in?

It's di-re (dire) that you let me in!

A HUSH puppy!

Bye (buy) some candy from me for our charity?